READY, STEADY, PRACTISE!

Paul Broadbent

Mental Arithmetic
Pupil Book Year 3

Features of this book

- Clear explanations and worked examples for each mental arithmetic topic from the KS2 National Curriculum.

- Questions split into three sections that become progressively more challenging:

Warm up

Test yourself

Challenge yourself

- 'How did you do?' checks at the end of each topic for self-evaluation.

- Regular progress tests to assess pupils' understanding and recap on their learning.

- Answers to every question in a pull-out section at the centre of the book.

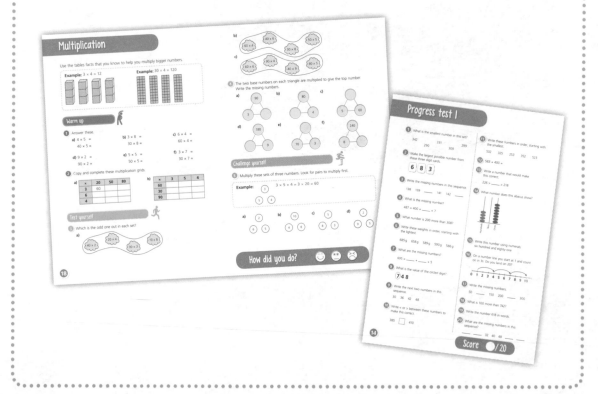

Contents

Counting and numbers

Some sequences have missing numbers. Look carefully at the numbers you are given and try to work out the numbers next to these first. Then you can write the others.

Example:

207   208   ___   ___   ___   212   ___

The missing numbers are 209, 210, 211 and 213.

Counting patterns can use steps of different numbers. To work out the steps, look at the difference between the numbers.

Example:

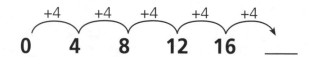

This is going up in multiples of four. The next number is 20.

Warm up

1 Copy each sequence and write the missing numbers.

a) 93   94   ___   ___   97   98   ___

b) 108   ___   110   111   ___   ___   114

c) ___   ___   381   382   ___   384   385

d) 703   704   705   ___   ___   ___   709

e) 596   597   ___   ___   ___   601   602

2 Write the next number in each of these sequences.

a) 22   24   26   28   30

b) 120   130   140   150   160

c) 32   36   40   44   48

d) 150   200   250   300   350

e) 8   16   24   32   40

3 Copy and complete these sequences.

    a) ____   ____   36   39   42   ____   ____

    b) ____   ____   60   70   80   ____   ____

    c) ____   ____   36   40   44   ____   ____

    d) ____   ____   24   32   40   ____   ____

4 The arrows show missing numbers. What are the missing numbers in these number lines?

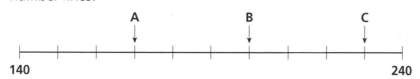

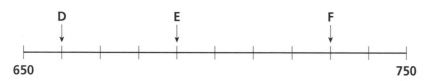

5 Write down the next three numbers in each of these sequences.

    a) 310   410   510   610

    b) 560   570   580   590

    c) 245   345   445   545

    d) 244   254   264   274

6 On a number track, I start at 5 and count on in 3s.

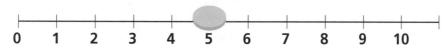

Will I land on 15?

7 Grace has between 20 and 30 books. She counted them in threes and there was 1 left over. She then counted them in fours and there was still 1 left over. How many books did she have in total?

How did you do?

Place value

Look at this number and how it is made.

562 = 500 + 60 + 2

five hundred and sixty-two

Hundreds	Tens	Ones
5	6	2

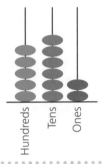

Make sure you look at the place of each digit in a number.

For example, 562 is very different from 625, even though it has the same digits.

Warm up

1 Find the missing numbers.

a) 285 ⟶ 200 + _____ + 5

b) 617 ⟶ _____ + 10 + 7

c) 354 ⟶ 300 + _____ + _____

d) 793 ⟶ _____ + _____ + 3

e) 198 ⟶ _____ + 90 + _____

2 Write these numbers as numerals.

a) six hundred and thirty-eight

b) four hundred and seventeen

c) seven hundred and eighty

d) five hundred and three

3 What numbers do these sets of arrow cards produce?

a)  400 30 7

b) 600 90 4

c)  900 10 8

d) 100 80 9

4 Answer these questions.

a) What number is 200 more than 525?   b) What number is 60 more than 418?

c) What number is 500 less than 803?   d) What number is 70 less than 497?

5 Write the numbers shown by each abacus.

a)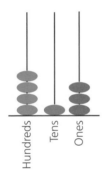
Hundreds Tens Ones

b)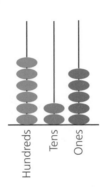
Hundreds Tens Ones

c)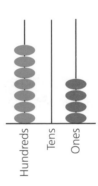
Hundreds Tens Ones

6 Numbers can be partitioned in different ways. What are the missing numbers?

a) **58**

    50 + 8

    40 + 18

    30 + ____

    ____ + 38

    10 + ____

b) **63**

    60 + 3

    50 + ____

    ____ + 23

    30 + ____

    ____ + 43

    10 + ____

c) **47**

    40 + ____

    ____ + 17

    20 + ____

    ____ + 37

How did you do?

Comparing and ordering numbers

< and > are used to compare numbers. Don't get them confused!

< means 'is less than'

Example: 135 < 214

135 is less than 214

> means 'is greater than'

Example: 368 > 309

368 is greater than 309

When you compare two numbers, you must look carefully at the value of the digits.

If you have a list of numbers to put in order, look at the place value of the digits, starting with the hundreds.

Example: Put these in order, starting with the smallest.

345　630　92　354　85　⟶　85　92　345　354　630

Warm up

1 Copy the numbers and write < or > between them to make these correct.

a) 75 ☐ 83

b) 212 ☐ 209

c) 395 ☐ 299

d) 507 ☐ 509

2 Look at this set of numbers. Which is the smallest number? Which is the largest number?

357　283　238　537　382　573

3 Write each set of numbers in order of size, starting with the smallest.

a) | 258 | 302 | 285 | 311 |

b) | 568 | 600 | 589 | 509 |

c) | 677 | 784 | 721 | 729 |

d) | 476 | 467 | 674 | 647 |

4 Write any number that would be correct for these.

a) 54 > _____ > 38

b) 106 > _____ > 93

c) 245 < _____ < 290

d) 512 < _____ < 515

Challenge yourself

5 Here are the lengths of six of the longest rivers in the UK. Copy the table and write the rivers in order, starting with the longest.

River Clyde 172 km

River Thames 346 km

River Severn 354 km

River Trent 297 km

River Tay 188 km

River Wye 215 km

Name of river	Length (km)

How did you do?

Addition

When you do addition with large numbers, break numbers up so that you can add them in your head.

Example: What is 158 add 5?

158 + 5
= 100 + 50 + 8 + 5
= 150 + 13 = 163

Add the ones and then add this to the hundreds and tens.

Example: Add together 233 and 40.

233 + 40
= 200 + 30 + 3 + 40
= 200 + 30 + 40 + 3
= 200 + 70 + 3 = 273

Add the tens and then add this to the hundreds and then add on the ones.

Warm up

1 Add these mentally and write the answers.

a) 83 + 5 =

b) 27 + 6 =

c) 53 + 9 =

d) 91 + 5 =

e) 142 + 3 =

f) 229 + 6 =

g) 234 + 7 =

h) 348 + 9 =

2 Now add these mentally and write the answers.

a) 31 + 50 =

b) 64 + 30 =

c) 23 + 70 =

d) 51 + 40 =

e) 234 + 40 =

f) 127 + 50 =

g) 201 + 90 =

h) 329 + 60 =

Test yourself

3 Copy and complete these addition grids.

a)

+	30	60	20	50
134	164			
211				
302				

b)

+	200	300	500	400
123	323			
307				
528				

4 Write the odd one out in each set.

a)

305 + 20   320 + 5   300 + 25   350 + 20

b)

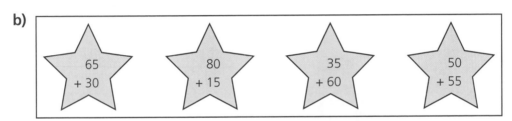

65 + 30   80 + 15   35 + 60   50 + 55

c)

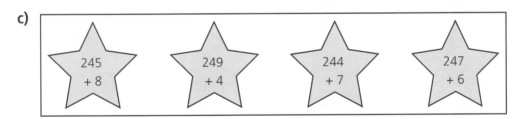

245 + 8   249 + 4   244 + 7   247 + 6

Challenge yourself

5 Two numbers total 105. One of the numbers is 95. What is the other number?

How did you do?

Subtraction

When you subtract large numbers, break numbers up so that you can subtract them in your head.

Example: What is 136 subtract 7?

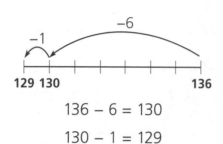

136 – 6 = 130

130 – 1 = 129

Subtract back to the next ten and then count back.

Example: Take away 30 from 155.

155 – 30

= **150 + 5** – 30

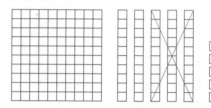

= 150 – 30 = 120 + **5** = 125

Subtract the hundreds and tens and then add on the ones.

Warm up

1 Subtract back to the next ten and then count back.

a) 148 – 9 =   b) 125 – 8 =

c) 163 – 6 =   d) 171 – 5 =

e) 182 – 7 =   f) 198 – 9 =

2 Break up the numbers and then subtract carefully.

a) 145 – 20 =   b) 138 – 30 =

c) 179 – 50 =   d) 165 – 40 =

e) 192 – 40 =   f) 154 – 50 =

Test yourself

3 Answer these.

a) Take 30 away from 74.   b) Subtract 60 from 130.

c) What is 300 less than 455?   d) Take away 9 from 160.

e) What is 186 take away 50?

4 Write the difference between each pair of numbers.

a)

130	200

b)

190	50

c)

140	90

d)

70	160

e)

80	190

f)

170	80

5 Copy and complete each chart to show the numbers coming out of each subtraction machine.

a)

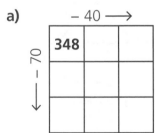

IN → −60 → OUT

IN	140	170	120	110	150	130
OUT	80					

b)

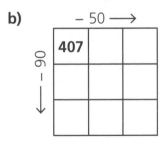

IN → −200 → OUT

IN	410	465	372	845	503	283
OUT	210					

Challenge yourself

6 Copy and complete these tables.

a)

− 40 ⟶

↓ − 70

348		

b)

− 50 ⟶

↓ − 90

407		

How did you do?

1 What is the smallest number in this set?

342   331   299
      290   309

2 Make the largest possible number from these three digit cards.

6 **8** **3**

3 Write the missing numbers in this sequence.

138   139   _____   141   142   _____

4 What is the missing number?

487 = 400 + _____ + 7

5 What number is 200 more than 308?

6 Write these weights in order, starting with the lightest.

685 g   658 g   589 g   590 g   586 g

7 What are the missing numbers?

695 = _____ + _____ + 5

8 What is the value of the circled digit?

⑦4 8

9 Write the next two numbers in this sequence.

30   36   42   48

10 Write < or > between these numbers to make this correct.

385 ☐ 410

11 Write these numbers in order, starting with the smallest.

532   325   253   352   523

12 583 + 400 =

13 Write a number that would make this correct.

226 > _____ > 218

14 What number does this abacus show?

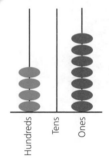

15 Write this number using numerals: six hundred and eighty-one

16 On a number line you start at 1 and count on in 3s. Do you land on 20?

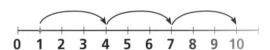

0 1 2 3 4 5 6 7 8 9 10

17 Write the missing numbers.

50   _____   150   200   _____   300

18 What is 100 more than 742?

19 Write the number 618 in words.

20 What are the missing numbers in this sequence?

_____   _____   32   40   48   _____   _____

Score ⬤/20

1 336 + 60 =

2 542 − 40 =

3 Copy and complete this addition grid.

+	48	99	54
7	55		

4 What number is 300 more than 654?

5 Two numbers have a difference of 20. One of the numbers is 78. What two numbers could the other number be?

6 What is the total of 483 and 400?

7 Copy and complete the chart to show the numbers coming out of this subtraction machine.

IN	161	56	117
OUT	153		

8 What is the missing number?

110 − _____ = 60

9 Which subtraction is the odd one out?

(79 − 3)   (72 − 5)

(73 − 6)   (71 − 4)

10 Add this mentally.

182 + 9 =

11 What is the missing number?

_____ + 80 = 94

12 Copy and complete this addition grid.

+	208	412	597
300	508		

13 645 − 200 =

14 Write down pairs of numbers that have a difference of 50.

(60)   (90)   (110)

(40)   (130)   (80)

15 Subtract 30 from 78.

16 Copy and complete the chart to show the numbers coming out of this subtraction machine.

IN	766	504	829
OUT	466		

17 What number is 200 less than 608?

18 259 − 40 =

19 Which is the odd one out?

(213 + 7)   (190 + 30)

(217 + 5)   (170 + 50)

20 I am thinking of a number. If I added 50 to the number, it would make 380. What number am I thinking of?

Multiplication facts

Look at these multiplication facts.

The 3 times table has an interesting pattern. The digits in the product always add up to 3, 6 or 9.

3 × 1 = 3	3 × 7 = 21
3 × 2 = 6	3 × 8 = 24
3 × 3 = 9	3 × 9 = 27
3 × 4 = 12	3 × 10 = 30
3 × 5 = 15	3 × 11 = 33
3 × 6 = 18	3 × 12 = 36

The 8 times table is double the 4 times table. The product is always an even number.

8 × 1 = 8	8 × 7 = 56
8 × 2 = 16	8 × 8 = 64
8 × 3 = 24	8 × 9 = 72
8 × 4 = 32	8 × 10 = 80
8 × 5 = 40	8 × 11 = 88
8 × 6 = 48	8 × 12 = 96

Warm up

1 Write the answers to these multiplications. Use the images to help you.

a) ☆☆☆☆☆☆
☆☆☆☆☆☆
☆☆☆☆☆☆

6 × 3 =
3 × 6 =

b) ☆☆☆☆☆☆☆☆
☆☆☆☆☆☆☆☆
☆☆☆☆☆☆☆☆
☆☆☆☆☆☆☆☆

8 × 4 =
4 × 8 =

c) ☆☆☆☆☆☆
☆☆☆☆☆☆
☆☆☆☆☆☆
☆☆☆☆☆☆
☆☆☆☆☆☆
☆☆☆☆☆☆
☆☆☆☆☆☆
☆☆☆☆☆☆

6 × 8 =
8 × 6 =

d) ☆☆☆☆☆
☆☆☆☆☆
☆☆☆☆☆
☆☆☆☆☆
☆☆☆☆☆
☆☆☆☆☆
☆☆☆☆☆
☆☆☆☆☆

5 × 8 =
8 × 5 =

e) ☆☆☆☆☆☆☆☆☆
☆☆☆☆☆☆☆☆☆
☆☆☆☆☆☆☆☆☆

9 × 3 =
3 × 9 =

f) ☆☆☆☆☆☆☆☆☆☆☆
☆☆☆☆☆☆☆☆☆☆☆
☆☆☆☆☆☆☆☆☆☆☆

3 × 11 =
11 × 3 =

2 Write four different multiplication facts for each number. Use the beads to help you.

a)

24

b)

48

c)

36

3 Use doubling to answer these.

a) 5 × 2 =

5 × 4 =

5 × 8 =

b) 7 × 2 =

7 × 4 =

7 × 8 =

c) 4 × 2 =

4 × 4 =

4 × 8 =

d) 6 × 2 =

6 × 4 =

6 × 8 =

e) 12 × 2 =

12 × 4 =

12 × 8 =

f) 9 × 2 =

9 × 4 =

9 × 8 =

Challenge yourself

4 Copy and complete these. Circle the answers you know instantly.

a) 8 × 2 =

b) 4 × 10 =

c) 5 × 9 =

d) 7 × 3 =

e) 3 × 6 =

f) 9 × 2 =

g) 8 × 4 =

h) 10 × 7 =

i) 7 × 8 =

j) 3 × 2 =

k) 9 × 3 =

l) 6 × 6 =

m) 9 × 5 =

n) 8 × 3 =

o) 4 × 9 =

p) 6 × 4 =

How did you do?

Multiplication

Use the tables facts that you know to help you multiply bigger numbers.

Example: 3 × 4 = 12

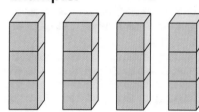

Example: 30 × 4 = 120

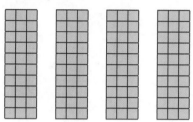

Warm up

1 Answer these.

a) 4 × 5 =   **b)** 3 × 8 =   **c)** 6 × 4 =
   40 × 5 =   30 × 8 =   60 × 4 =

d) 9 × 2 =   **e)** 5 × 5 =   **f)** 3 × 7 =
   90 × 2 =   50 × 5 =   30 × 7 =

2 Copy and complete these multiplication grids.

a)

×	20	50	80
3	60		
6			
4			

b)

×	3	5	4
60			
30			
90			

Test yourself

3 Which is the odd one out in each set?

a)

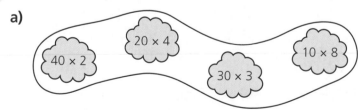

b)

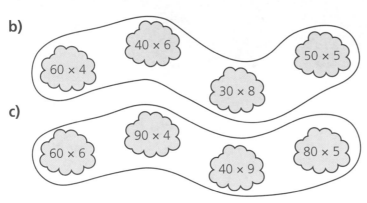

c)

4 The two base numbers on each triangle are multiplied to give the top number. Write the missing numbers.

a)
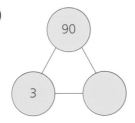

b)
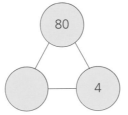

c)
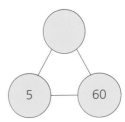

d)
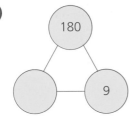

e)
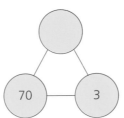

f)
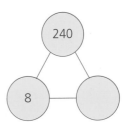

Challenge yourself

5 Multiply these sets of three numbers. Look for pairs to multiply first.

Example: **3 × 5 × 4 = 3 × 20 = 60**

a)

b)

c)

d)

How did you do?

Division

Look at these division examples.

What is 18 divided by 3?

Here are 18 counters divided into 3s.

This shows that there are 6 groups.

$18 \div 3 = 6$

What is 22 divided by 4?

Here are 22 counters divided into 4s.

This shows that there are 5 groups with 2 counters left over.

$22 \div 4 = 5$ remainder 2

Warm up

1 Write the answers.

a) ☆☆☆☆☆☆☆☆
☆☆☆☆☆☆☆☆
☆☆☆☆☆☆☆☆

$24 \div 3 =$

b) ☆☆☆☆☆☆☆
☆☆☆☆☆☆☆
☆☆☆☆☆☆☆
☆☆☆☆☆☆☆

$28 \div 4 =$

c) ☆☆☆☆☆☆☆☆☆
☆☆☆☆☆☆☆☆☆
☆☆☆☆☆☆☆☆☆

$27 \div 3 =$

d) ☆☆☆☆☆☆☆☆☆☆☆☆
☆☆☆☆☆☆☆☆☆☆☆☆
☆☆☆☆☆☆☆☆☆☆☆☆

$36 \div 3 =$

e) ☆☆☆☆☆☆☆☆☆☆☆
☆☆☆☆☆☆☆☆☆☆☆
☆☆☆☆☆☆☆☆☆☆☆
☆☆☆☆☆☆☆☆☆☆☆

$44 \div 4 =$

f) ☆☆☆☆☆☆☆☆
☆☆☆☆☆☆☆☆
☆☆☆☆☆☆☆☆
☆☆☆☆☆☆☆☆

$32 \div 4 =$

2 Copy and complete each chart to show the numbers coming out of each division machine.

a)

IN → ÷5 → OUT

IN	30	50	80	100	70	60
OUT	6					

b)

IN → ÷10 → OUT

IN	90	120	150	200	180	170
OUT	9					

3 Copy these divisions, then write down the remainder for each division from the options below.

a) (28 ÷ 3)   **b)** (36 ÷ 2)   **c)** (55 ÷ 10)

       d) (39 ÷ 5)   **e)** (43 ÷ 4)   **f)** (42 ÷ 5)

no remainder	1	2	3	4	5

4 Divide these and write the answers and remainders.

a)

49 → ÷ 4 = __ r __

49 → ÷ 10 = __ r __

→ ÷ 2 = __ r __

b)

44 → ÷ 5 = __ r __

44 → ÷ 3 = __ r __

→ ÷ 10 = __ r __

How did you do?

Addition and subtraction problems

Look out for addition and subtraction words in any problems. They can give a clue for how to solve the problem.

Addition words

add, total, altogether, sum, plus, more than, increase

Subtraction words

subtract, take away, minus, less than, fewer, difference, reduce

Be careful. Some problems can be confusing. Read them carefully and 'picture' the problem.

Example: Two mobile phones have a difference in price of £30. The more expensive one costs £120. How much is the cheaper one?

£120 − £30 = £90

Warm up

1. **a)** A loaf of bread costs 80p. It is reduced in price by 15p.

   What is the cost of the loaf now?

   b) There are 200 children in Sam's school and 190 children in Joel's school.

   How many children are there in total in the two schools?

   c) A lorry travels 35 km to collect boxes of vegetables from a farm and 60 km to the town market.

   How far does the lorry travel altogether?

   d) Becky scored 145 points on a computer game. Hannah scored 8 fewer points than Becky.

   How many points did Hannah score?

   e) Dan buys shoes for £28 and a coat for £40.

   How much does he spend altogether?

   f) The difference in length between two sticks is 12 cm.

   If the longer stick is 50 cm, how long is the shorter stick?

Answers

Pages 4–5
1. **a)** 95, 96, 99   **b)** 109, 112, 113
   c) 379, 380, 383   **d)** 706, 707, 708
   e) 598, 599, 600
2. **a)** 32   **b)** 170
   c) 52   **d)** 400
   e) 48
3. **a)** 30, 33, 45, 48   **b)** 40, 50, 90, 100
   c) 28, 32, 48, 52   **d)** 8, 16, 48, 56
4. **A** 170   **B** 200   **C** 230
   D 660   **E** 690   **F** 730
5. **a)** 710, 810, 910   **b)** 600, 610, 620
   c) 645, 745, 845   **d)** 284, 294, 304
6. No
7. 25

Pages 6–7
1. **a)** 80   **b)** 600
   c) 50, 4   **d)** 700, 90
   e) 100, 8
2. **a)** 638   **b)** 417   **c)** 780   **d)** 503
3. **a)** 437   **b)** 694   **c)** 918   **d)** 189
4. **a)** 725   **b)** 478   **c)** 303   **d)** 427
5. **a)** 413   **b)** 625   **c)** 704
6. **a)** 58 → 30 + 28, 20 + 38, 10 + 48
   b) 63 → 50 + 13, 40 + 23, 30 + 33, 20 + 43,
   10 + 53
   c) 47 → 40 + 7, 30 + 17, 20 + 27, 10 + 37

Pages 8–9
1. **a)** <   **b)** >   **c)** >   **d)** <
2. 238, (573)
3. **a)** 258, 285, 302, 311   **b)** 509, 568, 589, 600
   c) 677, 721, 729, 784   **d)** 467, 476, 647, 674
4. **a)** Any number between 38 and 54
   b) Any number between 93 and 106
   c) Any number between 245 and 290
   d) 513 or 514
5. Rivers should be listed in this order: River Severn –
   354 km; River Thames – 346 km; River Trent –
   297 km; River Wye – 215 km; River Tay – 188 km;
   River Clyde – 172 km

Pages 10–11
1. **a)** 88   **b)** 33   **c)** 62   **d)** 96
   e) 145   **f)** 235   **g)** 241   **h)** 357
2. **a)** 81   **b)** 94   **c)** 93   **d)** 91
   e) 274   **f)** 177   **g)** 291   **h)** 389
3. **a)**

+	30	60	20	50
134	164	194	154	184
211	241	271	231	261
302	332	362	322	352

b)

+	200	300	500	400
123	323	423	623	523
307	507	607	807	707
528	728	828	1028	928

4. **a)** 350 + 20   **b)** 50 + 55   **c)** 244 + 7
5. 10

Pages 12–13
1. **a)** 139   **b)** 117   **c)** 157   **d)** 166   **e)** 175   **f)** 189
2. **a)** 125   **b)** 108   **c)** 129
   d) 125   **e)** 152   **f)** 104
3. **a)** 44   **b)** 70   **c)** 155
   d) 151   **e)** 136
4. **a)** 70   **b)** 140   **c)** 50
   d) 90   **e)** 110   **f)** 90
5. **a)** Bottom row should be completed as follows:
   110, 60, 50, 90, 70
   b) Bottom row should be completed as follows:
   265, 172, 645, 303, 83
6. **a)**

− 40 →		
348	308	268
278	238	198
208	168	128

−70↓

b)

− 50 →		
407	357	307
317	267	217
227	177	127

−90↓

Page 14
1. 290
2. 863
3. 140, 143
4. 80
5. 508
6. 586 g, 589 g, 590 g,
   658 g, 685 g
7. 600, 90
8. 700
9. 54, 60
10. <
11. 253, 325, 352, 523,
    532
12. 983
13. Any one of: 219, 220,
    221, 222, 223, 224,
    225
14. 407
15. 681
16. No
17. 100, 250
18. 842
19. Six hundred and
    eighteen
20. 16, 24, 56, 64

Answers

Page 15

1. 396
2. 502
3. 106, 61
4. 954
5. 58 or 98
6. 883
7. 48, 109
8. 50
9. 79 – 3
10. 191
11. 14
12. 712, 897
13. 445
14. 130 and 80, 60 and 110, 90 and 40
15. 48
16. 204, 529
17. 408
18. 219
19. 217 + 5
20. 330

Pages 16–17

1. a) 18, 18   b) 32, 32   c) 48, 48
   d) 40, 40   e) 27, 27   f) 33, 33
2. a) Any four of these: 3 × 8, 8 × 3, 6 × 4, 4 × 6, 2 × 12, 12 × 2, 1 × 24, 24 × 1
   b) Any four of these: 4 × 12, 12 × 4, 8 × 6, 6 × 8, 3 × 16, 16 × 3, 24 × 2, 2 × 24, 1 × 48, 48 × 1
   c) Any four of these: 6 × 6, 9 × 4, 4 × 9, 3 × 12, 12 × 3, 2 × 18, 18 × 2, 1 × 36, 36 × 1
3. a) 10, 20, 40   b) 14, 28, 56
   c) 8, 16, 32   d) 12, 24, 48
   e) 24, 48, 96   f) 18, 36, 72
4. a) 16   b) 40
   c) 45   d) 21
   e) 18   f) 18
   g) 32   h) 70
   i) 56   j) 6
   k) 27   l) 36
   m) 45   n) 24
   o) 36   p) 24

Pages 18–19

1. a) 20, 200   b) 24, 240
   c) 24, 240   d) 18, 180
   e) 25, 250   f) 21, 210
2. a)

×	20	50	80
3	60	150	240
6	120	300	480
4	80	200	320

   b)

×	3	5	4
60	180	300	240
30	90	150	120
90	270	450	360

3. a) 30 × 3   b) 50 × 5   c) 80 × 5
4. a) 30   b) 20   c) 300
   d) 20   e) 210   f) 30
5. a) 60   b) 240
   c) 120   d) 90

Pages 20–21

1. a) 8   b) 7   c) 9
   d) 12   e) 11   f) 8
2. a) Bottom row should be completed as follows:
      10, 16, 20, 14, 12
   b) Bottom row should be completed as follows:
      12, 15, 20, 18, 17
3. a) r1
   b) r0
   c) r5
   d) r4
   e) r3
   f) r2
4. a) 12 r 1, 4 r 9, 24 r 1
   b) 8 r 4, 14 r 2, 4 r 4

Pages 22–23

1. a) 65p   b) 390 children
   c) 95 km   d) 137 points
   e) £68   f) 38 cm
2. a) Monday → 200
      Tuesday → 240
      Wednesday → 190
      Footballs → 170
      Basketballs → 160
      Tennis balls → 300
      Total → 630
   b) 140   c) 40
3. a) 40 miles   b) 29 miles
   c) 7 miles   d) 33 miles
   e) 5 miles

Pages 24–25

1. a) £120   b) 3
   c) 100   d) 4
   e) £28   f) 8
2. a) Melon   b) Orange
   c) Mango   d) Guava
3. 37

Pages 26–27

1. a) 240   b) 7
   c) 120   d) 3
   e) 48   f) 12
   g) 16   h) 48
2.

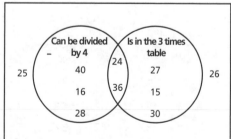

3. a) 12   b) 6
   c) 4   d) 3
   e) 2

4. a) 45, 25   b) 45, 60, 30
    c) 45, 25   d) 80, 30
    e) 80

5. 90 g, 110 g

6. **4** × **6** = 24 (or **6** × **4** = 24), **27** ÷ 3 = 9, **3** × 5 = **15**, 30 ÷ **5** = 6

7. 15

Page 28

1.	3 × 6 or 6 × 3	**10.**	r 2
2.	45	**11.**	160
3.	5	**12.**	56 ÷ 7
4.	2, 3, 4, 6, 8	**13.**	70
5.	16, 32, 64	**14.**	50
6.	16	**15.**	300
7.	200	**16.**	25 ÷ 7 and 20 ÷ 8
8.	18	**17.**	8
9.	9 × 4 and 6 × 6; 3 × 8 and 4 × 6; 8 × 2 and 4 × 4	**18.**	360
		19.	5 r 3
		20.	49, 490

Page 29

1.	155 km	**12.**	89p
2.	150	**13.**	30
3.	24	**14.**	8
4.	200 m	**15.**	124 cm
5.	480	**16.**	44 p
6.	32	**17.**	23
7.	72	**18.**	8
8.	63	**19.**	6
9.	54	**20.**	14 and 10
10.	30 km		
11.	189		

Pages 30–31

1. a) $\frac{3}{4}$ b) $\frac{1}{6}$
    c) $\frac{5}{8}$ d) $\frac{2}{5}$

2. a) $\frac{1}{3}, \frac{2}{6}$ b) $\frac{3}{4}, \frac{9}{12}$
    c) $\frac{1}{2}, \frac{5}{10}$ d) $\frac{2}{5}, \frac{4}{10}$

3. a) $\frac{1}{2} = \frac{2}{4} = \frac{3}{6} = \frac{4}{8} = \frac{5}{10} = \frac{6}{12}$
    b) $\frac{1}{3} = \frac{2}{6} = \frac{3}{9} = \frac{4}{12} = \frac{5}{15} = \frac{6}{18}$
    c) $\frac{1}{4} = \frac{2}{8} = \frac{3}{12} = \frac{4}{16} = \frac{5}{20} = \frac{6}{24}$
    d) $\frac{1}{5} = \frac{2}{10} = \frac{3}{15} = \frac{4}{20} = \frac{5}{25} = \frac{6}{30}$

Pages 32–33

1. a) 3   b) 2
    c) 5   d) 4

2. a) 7   b) 10
    c) 7   d) 5
    e) 7   f) 11

3. a) i) $\frac{1}{5}$ of 20 = 4   ii) $\frac{1}{2}$ of 20 = 10   iii) $\frac{1}{4}$ of 20 = 5
    b) so $\frac{1}{2}$

4. True

5. a) <   b) >
    c) >   d) >
    e) <   f) >

6. 6 chickens, 8 goats, 10 ducks

Pages 34–35

1. a) $\frac{4}{10}$, 0.4   b) $1\frac{5}{10}$, 1.5
    c) $2\frac{1}{10}$, 2.1

2. a) $\frac{2}{4}$ (or $\frac{1}{2}$)   b) $\frac{2}{6}$ (or $\frac{1}{3}$)
    c) $\frac{4}{10}$ (or $\frac{2}{5}$)   d) $\frac{4}{5}$

3. a) $\frac{3}{3}$ or 1   b) $\frac{4}{4}$ or 1
    c) $\frac{2}{2}$ or 1   d) $\frac{5}{5}$ or 1

    All answers equal 1.

4. $\frac{1}{6}, \frac{1}{4}, \frac{1}{3}, \frac{1}{2}, \frac{2}{3}, \frac{3}{4}$

Pages 36–37

1. 1 m 25 cm → 125 cm
    1 m 20 cm → 120 cm
    120 mm → 12 cm
    3 m → 300 cm
    300 mm → 30 cm
    3 cm → 30 mm

2. a) >   b) =
    c) >   d) <
    e) >   f) =

3. a) 9 kg   b) 12 kg 500 g
    c) 11 kg 500 g   d) 17 kg 500 g

4. a) 5   b) 20
    c) 4   d) 20
    e) 4

5. Three 50 cm and two 90 cm length pipes

Pages 38–39

1. a) 97p   b) 79p   c) 71p

2. a) Two 20p and two 5p coins or one 20p and three 10p coins
    b) One 10p and one 50p coins
    c) One 50p, one 10p, two 2p and one 1p coins or two 20p, two 10p and one 5p coins

3. a) 50p, 20p, 10p, 5p coins
    b) £1, 20p, 2p, 2p coins
    c) 50p, 20p, 20p, 5p, 2p, 2p coins

4. 20p

5. a) £4   b) £3
    c) £2   d) £6

6. a) £12   b) £36
    c) £45   d) £18
    e) 8

Pages 40–41

1. a) 3.10   b) 4.26
    c) 9.35   d) 11.30
    e) 1.40   f) 2.19
    g) 10.15   h) 5.05

Answers

2. **a)** afternoon   **b)** morning   **c)** morning
    d) morning   **e)** afternoon   **f)** evening

3. **a)** 6.55   **b)** 9.40
    c) 2.10   **d)** 11.25

4. **a)** 2 minutes   **b)** 21 days
    c) 240 minutes   **d)** 2 weeks
    e) 150 seconds   **f)** 90 minutes
    g) 48 months   **h)** 10 hours

Page 42

1. $\frac{3}{8}$

2. Any two parts shaded

3. $\frac{2}{4}$

4. $\frac{4}{12}$

5. 5

6. <

7. 0.3

8. $\frac{5}{9}$

9. $\frac{2}{12}$

10. Any two parts shaded

11. $\frac{4}{10}$, 0.4

12. $\frac{1}{6}, \frac{1}{4}, \frac{1}{3}, \frac{1}{2}$

13. $\frac{4}{5}$

14. True

15. $\frac{2}{10}, \frac{3}{15}$

16. 5

17. 18

18. 12

19. 6

20. 9

Page 43

1. 4

2. £1.20

3. 6

4. £1.10

5. £2

6. 90p

7. 11.25

8. 50p, 20p, 20p, 5p

9. 1500 g

10. 7 kg, $3\frac{1}{2}$ kg

11. 450 cm

12. =, <

13. 10p, 10p, 5p

14. 10.20, 4.35

15. 400 cm

16. 29p

17. 2 kg 500 g

18. 2 weeks

19. 2.55

20. 18 cm

2 This table shows the number of balls made in a factory over three days.

a) Complete the totals.

	Footballs	Basketballs	Tennis balls	Total number of balls
Monday	40	60	100	____
Tuesday	70	50	120	____
Wednesday	60	50	80	____
Total of each ball	____	____	____	____

b) How many more tennis balls than basketballs were made in total?

c) How many fewer balls were made on Monday than on Tuesday?

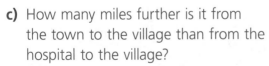 **Challenge yourself**

3 Look at the map and answer these questions.

a) On Tuesday the doctor drives from the town to the village and then on to the school.

How many miles does the doctor travel?

b) A bus goes from the town to the hospital and then to the village.

How many miles does the bus travel on this journey in total?

c) How many miles further is it from the town to the village than from the hospital to the village?

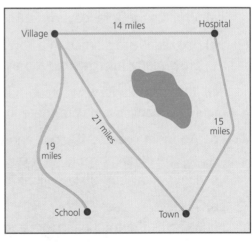

d) On Wednesday the doctor travels from the hospital to the village and then drives on to the school. How many miles does he travel altogether?

e) How many more miles is it from the school to the village than from the hospital to the village?

Multiplication and division problems

Look out for multiplication and division words in any problems. They can give a clue for how to solve the problem.

Multiplication words

multiply, times, product, groups of, sets of

Division words

divide, group, share, fraction, remainder

Always look carefully to see if your answer makes sense. When you divide and there is a remainder, check to see if the answer should be rounded up or down.

Example: Oranges are put in bags, with six oranges fitting in each bag. How many bags are needed for 20 oranges?

$20 \div 6 = 3$ remainder 2

This means that four bags are needed to hold all the oranges.

Warm up

1 Answer these problems.

a) What is the total cost of four lamps each costing £30?

b) Six beans are planted in a row. There are 20 beans in a packet. How many full rows can be planted from this pack of beans?

c) There are 25 jelly sweets in a bag. How many sweets are there in four bags?

d) A farmer collects 40 eggs and puts them into egg boxes that hold 12 eggs. All the eggs must be in an egg box. How many egg boxes will he need?

e) A cushion costs £7. What is the total price for four cushions?

f) A ribbon is 85 cm in length. How many 10 cm lengths can be made from this ribbon?

2 Answer these multiplications and divisions.

Find the matching code letter shown in the chart and the names of four fruits.

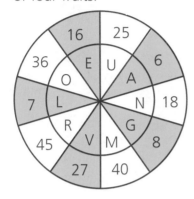

a) 5 × 8 = **40 M**

   4 × 4 =

   49 ÷ 7 =

   3 × 12 =

   9 × 2 =

b) 6 × 6 =

   9 × 5 =

   18 ÷ 3 =

   3 × 6 =

   32 ÷ 4 =

   2 × 8 =

c) 4 × 10 =

   54 ÷ 9 =

   9 × 2 =

   24 ÷ 3 =

   4 × 9 =

d) 2 × 4 =

   5 × 5 =

   24 ÷ 4 =

   3 × 9 =

   48 ÷ 8 =

Challenge yourself

3 James has a box of shells collected from the beach.
He knows he has between 30 and 40 shells but groups them to count them. He puts them into groups of three and has one shell left over. He tries again, putting them in groups of four this time, but he still has one left over.

How many shells does he have?

How did you do?

Mixed problems

Read each problem, diagram or puzzle carefully. Draw pictures or use objects to help if you are struggling to work it out in your head.

Warm up

1 Answer these problems.

    a) What is 40 multiplied by 6?

    b) How much more is 32 than 25?

    c) What number is 10 times greater than 12?

    d) What is the difference between 99 and 102?

    e) What is 12 multiplied by 4?

    f) What is 36 divided by 3?

    g) What number is 9 less than 25?

    h) What number when divided by 2 gives an answer of 24?

2 Copy this Venn diagram. Write these numbers in the correct part of your Venn diagram.

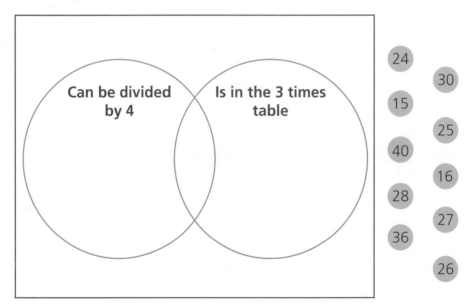

3 Look at this clock face. There are 60 minutes in one hour.

Answer these questions. Use the clock face to help you.

a) How many groups of 5 minutes are there in one hour?

b) How many groups of 10 minutes are there in one hour?

c) How many groups of 15 minutes are there in one hour?

d) How many groups of 20 minutes are there in one hour?

e) How many groups of 30 minutes are there in one hour?

4 Choose numbers from the five leaves to answer each question.

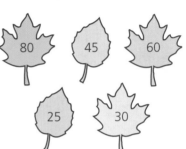

a) Which two numbers leave a remainder of 1 when divided by 2?

b) Which three numbers divide exactly by 3?

c) Which two numbers total 70?

d) Which two numbers have a difference of 50?

e) Which number is 4 × 4 × 5?

5 Two necklaces have a difference in weight of 20 g. When they are put together they have a total weight of 200 g. What is the weight of each necklace?

6 Use each of the digits 1–6 once only to copy and complete the calculations below.

| 1 | 2 | 3 | 4 | 5 | 6 |

 × = 24   ☐7 ÷ 3 = 9   ☐ × 5 = ☐5   30 ÷ ☐ = 6

7 Ali is making filled rolls in his sandwich shop. He has three different types of rolls and five different types of fillings. He only puts one filling into each roll.

How many different filled rolls can he sell?

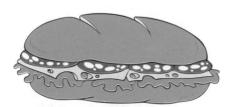

How did you do?

1 Copy and complete the multiplication fact shown.

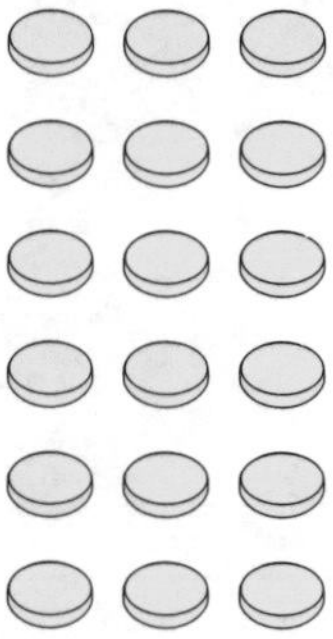

⬭ ⬭ ⬭
⬭ ⬭ ⬭
⬭ ⬭ ⬭
⬭ ⬭ ⬭
⬭ ⬭ ⬭
⬭ ⬭ ⬭

_____ × _____ = 18

2 $9 × 5 =$

3 $30 ÷ 6 =$

4 Write down the numbers shown below that divide exactly into 24.

② ④ ⑥ ⑧
③ ⑤ ⑦ ⑨

5 Write the answers for these.

$8 × 2 =$

$8 × 4 =$

$8 × 8 =$

6 $160 ÷ 10 =$

7 $40 × 5 =$

8 $90 ÷ 5 =$

9 Copy these numbers then join pairs of multiplications with the same answer.

$9 × 4$

$3 × 8$

$6 × 6$

$4 × 4$

$8 × 2$ $4 × 6$

10 What is the remainder when 30 is divided by 4?

11 $20 × 8 =$

12 Which division is the odd one out?

$42 ÷ 7$ $56 ÷ 7$

$48 ÷ 8$

$54 ÷ 9$

13 $5 × 7 × 2 =$

14 $250 ÷ 5 =$

15 Multiply 60 by 5.

16 Write down the two divisions with a remainder of 4.

$49 ÷ 6$

$38 ÷ 5$ $25 ÷ 7$

$54 ÷ 9$

$20 ÷ 8$

17 $56 ÷ 7 =$

18 A box holds 40 apples.
How many apples are there in nine boxes?

19 $43 ÷ 8 =$ ☐ r ☐

20 Answer these.

$7 × 7 =$

$7 × 70 =$

Score ◯ / 20

1 A lorry travels 85 km in the morning and 70 km in the afternoon. How many kilometres does the lorry travel altogether?

2 A teacher gives a daily tables test. There are 30 questions in each test. How many questions are there in total over five days?

3 There are 19 people on a bus. At a bus stop seven people get on the bus and two get off the bus.
How many people are on the bus now?

4 A swimming pool is 50 m long. Jess swims four lengths.
How many metres does she swim in total?

5 A book has 540 pages and I have read 60 pages. How many more pages will I need to read to finish the book?

> **Look at these numbers for questions 6–9.**
>
> 63   32   40   9

6 Which number leaves a remainder of 2 when divided by 5?

7 Add together the two even numbers.

8 Which number is 3 × 7 × 3?

9 What is the difference between the two odd numbers?

10 Alice travels 3 km to school and another 3 km home from school. She goes to school five days a week. How far does she travel in total in one week?

11 There are 196 children in a school. Today seven are absent.
How many children are in school today?

12 What is the total of 83p and 6p?

13 There are five pairs of socks in a pack and two single socks in each pair. How many single socks are there in three packs?

14 48 flowers are shared equally between six vases. How many are in each vase?

15 Jo is 50 cm shorter than her mum. Her mum is 174 cm tall. How tall is Jo?

16 What is the total cost of a 30p ruler and a 14p pencil?

17 A brown chicken laid 28 eggs in a month. A white chicken laid five fewer eggs than the brown chicken.
How many eggs did the white chicken lay?

> **Here are 24 beads. Use them to answer questions 18–20.**
>
>

18 All the beads are used to make three necklaces each with the same number of beads. How many are on each necklace?

19 There are four different colour beads: red, blue, green, yellow. There is the same number of beads of each colour.
How many red beads will there be?

20 Two necklaces are made using all the beads. One necklace has four more beads than the other.
How many beads are there on each necklace?

Score ⬤/20

Equivalent fractions

A fraction, such as $\frac{2}{3}$, has two parts.

The **denominator** tells you the number of equal parts the whole is divided into. → $\frac{2}{3}$ ← The **numerator** tells you the number of those equal parts that are taken.

This shows $\frac{2}{3}$.

This shows $\frac{4}{6}$.

These are **equivalent fractions**.

This fraction strip shows some equivalent fractions.

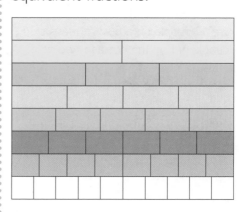

Use the strip to see that $\frac{1}{2}$ is the same as $\frac{2}{4}$ and $\frac{5}{10}$.

What else is $\frac{1}{2}$ equivalent to?

Warm up

1. What fraction of each of these shapes is shaded blue?

a)

b)

c)

d)

2 Write the pairs of equivalent fractions shaded blue for each shape.

a)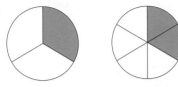

b)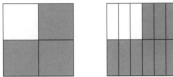

c)

d)

3 Copy and complete the next equivalent fraction in each of these.

a) $\dfrac{1}{2} = \dfrac{2}{\square} = \dfrac{\square}{6} = \dfrac{4}{\square} = \dfrac{\square}{\square} = \dfrac{\square}{\square}$

b) $\dfrac{1}{3} = \dfrac{\square}{6} = \dfrac{3}{\square} = \dfrac{\square}{12} = \dfrac{\square}{\square} = \dfrac{\square}{\square}$

c) $\dfrac{1}{4} = \dfrac{2}{\square} = \dfrac{\square}{12} = \dfrac{4}{\square} = \dfrac{\square}{\square} = \dfrac{\square}{\square}$

d) $\dfrac{1}{5} = \dfrac{\square}{10} = \dfrac{3}{\square} = \dfrac{\square}{20} = \dfrac{\square}{\square} = \dfrac{\square}{\square}$

How did you do?

Fractions of amounts

When you need to find fractions of amounts, use the numerator and denominator. When the numerator is 1, just divide the amount by the denominator.

Example: What is $\frac{1}{5}$ of 10?

Divide 10 into five groups.

$\frac{1}{5}$ of 10 = 2

Warm up

1 Work out $\frac{1}{4}$ of each group of fish.

a)

$\frac{1}{4}$ of 12 =

b)

$\frac{1}{4}$ of 8 =

c)

$\frac{1}{4}$ of 20 =

d)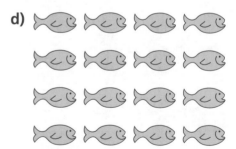

$\frac{1}{4}$ of 16 =

2 Answer these.

a) $\frac{1}{5}$ of 35 =

b) $\frac{1}{4}$ of 40 =

c) $\frac{1}{3}$ of 21 =

d) $\frac{1}{6}$ of 30 =

e) $\frac{1}{10}$ of 70 =

f) $\frac{1}{3}$ of 33 =

3 **a)** Here are 20 oranges. Answer these.

    i) $\frac{1}{5}$ of 20 =

    ii) $\frac{1}{2}$ of 20 =

    iii) $\frac{1}{4}$ of 20 =

b) Which would give you the greatest number of oranges,

    $\frac{1}{5}$, $\frac{1}{2}$ or $\frac{1}{4}$ of them?

4 Look at your answers to question 3. Is it true that $\frac{1}{2}$ is greater than $\frac{1}{4}$ and $\frac{1}{4}$ is greater than $\frac{1}{5}$?

5 Copy and complete these by writing < or > between each pair of amounts.

    a) $\frac{1}{6}$ of 30 ☐ $\frac{1}{5}$ of 30   **b)** $\frac{1}{3}$ of 15 ☐ $\frac{1}{5}$ of 15

    c) $\frac{1}{4}$ of 24 ☐ $\frac{1}{8}$ of 24   **d)** $\frac{1}{2}$ of 30 ☐ $\frac{1}{10}$ of 30

    e) $\frac{1}{10}$ of 40 ☐ $\frac{1}{5}$ of 40   **f)** $\frac{1}{3}$ of 18 ☐ $\frac{1}{6}$ of 18

6 Mr Jones has a total of 24 farm animals.

Write the number of each farm animal he owns.

$\frac{2}{8}$ are chickens = $\frac{2}{6}$ are goats =

$\frac{5}{12}$ are ducks =

How did you do?

Fractions

Fractions can be shown using a number line.

This number line is divided into tenths. They are written as common fractions (e.g. $\frac{1}{10}$) and as decimal fractions (e.g. 0.1).

$\frac{1}{10} = 0.1$ zero point one

$1\frac{2}{10} = 1.2$ one point two

The decimal point separates the whole number from the fraction.

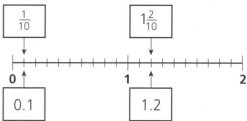

Warm up

1 The arrows on the number lines below indicate missing numbers.

Write both the common fraction and decimal fraction for each missing number.

Example:

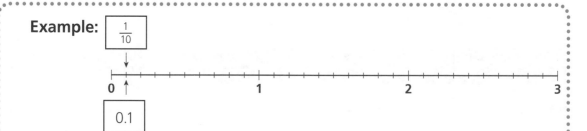

a)

b)

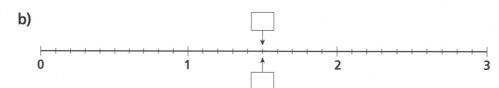

c)

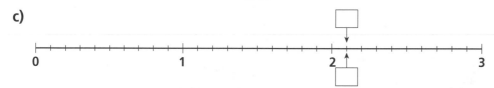

It is easy to add fractions with the same denominator – just add the numerators.

$\frac{1}{5}$ + $\frac{2}{5}$ = $\frac{3}{5}$

2 Add these fractions. Use the images to help you.

a) $\frac{1}{4} + \frac{1}{4} =$

b) $\frac{1}{6} + \frac{1}{6} =$

c)

$\frac{1}{10} + \frac{3}{10} =$ +

d) $\frac{1}{5} + \frac{3}{5} =$

3 Add these fractions. Use the images to help you. What do you notice?

a) $\frac{1}{3} + \frac{2}{3} =$

b) $\frac{1}{4} + \frac{3}{4} =$

c) $\frac{1}{2} + \frac{1}{2} =$ +

d) $\frac{2}{5} + \frac{3}{5} =$

4 Look at the fraction of each circle shaded red. Write these fractions in order, starting with the smallest.

$\frac{1}{2}$ $\frac{1}{4}$ $\frac{2}{3}$ $\frac{1}{3}$ $\frac{3}{4}$ $\frac{1}{6}$

How did you do?

Measures

You measure different things using different units.

Length

You measure the length of objects in millimetres (mm), centimetres (cm) and metres (m).

10 mm = 1 cm

100 cm = 1 m

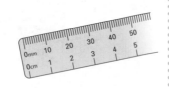

Capacity

You measure the capacity of containers in millilitres (ml) and litres (l).

1000 ml = 1 litres

Mass

You measure the mass or weight of an object in grams (g) and kilograms (kg).

1000 g = 1 kg

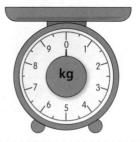

Warm up

1. Write the matching lengths.

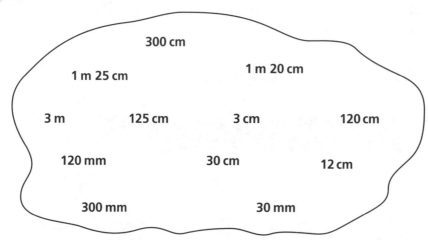

- 300 cm
- 1 m 25 cm
- 1 m 20 cm
- 3 m
- 125 cm
- 3 cm
- 120 cm
- 120 mm
- 30 cm
- 12 cm
- 300 mm
- 30 mm

2. Write the sign <, > or = between the measurements to make each of these true.

a) 1 m 65 cm ☐ 165 mm

b) 2 m 40 cm ☐ 240 cm

c) 200 mm ☐ 2 cm

d) 60 cm ☐ 6 m

e) 18 cm ☐ 80 mm

f) 5 m 30 cm ☐ 530 cm

3 Write the total mass of each of these using kilograms and grams.

a)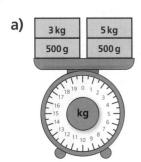

b)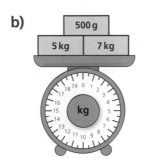

c)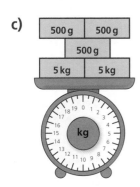

d)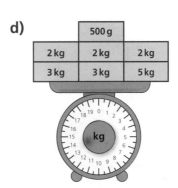

4 Write the answers.

   a) How many 200 ml bottles will fill a 1-litre jug?

   b) How many 100 ml cups will fill a 2-litre jug?

   c) How many 250 ml jugs will fill a 1-litre bottle?

   d) How many 5 ml teaspoons will fill a 100 ml cup?

   e) How many 500 ml bottles will fill a 2-litre jug?

Challenge yourself

5 Pipes come in two lengths: 50 cm and 90 cm long. They join together to make different lengths.

50 cm

90 cm

How many of each length would be needed to make a total length of exactly 3 m 30 cm? Draw a picture of joined pipes to show your answer.

How did you do?

Money

Look at these coins.

There are 100 pence in £1.

£1 = 100p

£2 = 200p

£1 and 50p = 150p

Warm up

1. How much money is in each purse?

a)

b)

c)

2. Answer these.

a) A pencil costs 50p and you use four coins to pay for it.
Which coins could you use?

b) A ball costs 80p and you have a 20p coin in your hand.
You use two more coins to make the total. Which coins did you use?

c) A balloon costs 75p and you have a 10p coin in your hand.
You use five more coins to make the total. Which coins did you use?

3 Make up the following amounts with the fewest number of coins.

a) 85p **b)** 124p **c)** 99p

4 Amy buys these three items.
What change will she get from £2?

5 What is the total cost of these items?

a)

One toothbrush costs 80p,
what do five toothbrushes cost?

b)

One toothpaste costs 60p,
what do five toothpastes cost?

c)

One soap costs 50p, what do
four soaps cost?

d)

One shower gel costs £2, what
do three shower gels cost?

Challenge yourself

6 Read the information and answer these questions.

> • A bus journey to the National Park costs £3.
> • Day tickets to the National Park cost £6.

a) How much does it cost for four people to travel on this bus?

b) How much does it cost for six people to visit the National Park?

c) How much does it cost for five people to catch the bus and also visit the park?

d) Children get into the National Park for half price. How much would it cost two adults and two children to visit the park?

e) An adult yearly pass to the park costs £48. How many times could you visit on a day ticket for the same price as the yearly pass?

How did you do?

Time

There are 60 minutes in one hour. It takes five minutes for the minute hand to move from one number to the next.

Example:

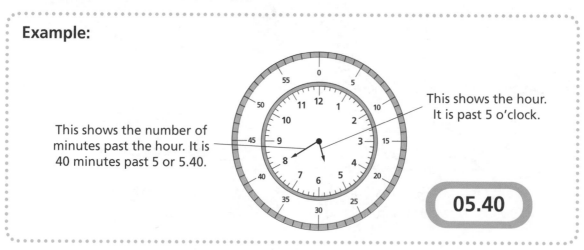

This shows the number of minutes past the hour. It is 40 minutes past 5 or 5.40.

This shows the hour. It is past 5 o'clock.

05.40

a.m. (ante meridiem) means before midday, so morning times.

p.m. (post meridiem) means after midday, so afternoon and evening times.

Warm up

1. Write the times shown on each clock face as in the example above.

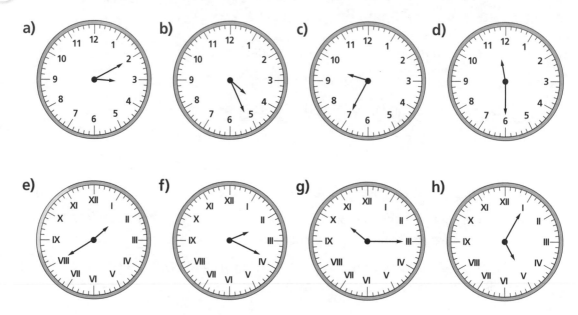

a) b) c) d)

e) f) g) h)

2 Are these times morning, afternoon or evening?

a) 4.05 p.m. **b)** 9.25 a.m. **c)** 11.45 a.m.

d) 8.50 a.m. **e)** 2.55 p.m. **f)** 7.45 p.m.

3 What is the time half an hour later than these clocks?

a)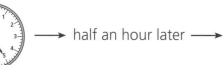

b)

c)

d)

4 Copy and complete these.

a) 120 seconds = _____ minutes   **b)** 3 weeks   = _____ days

c) 4 hours   = _____ minutes   **d)** 14 days   = _____ weeks

e) $2\frac{1}{2}$ minutes = _____ seconds   **f)** $1\frac{1}{2}$ hours   = _____ minutes

g) 4 years   = _____ months   **h)** 600 minutes = _____ hours

How did you do?

Progress test 5

1

What fraction of the rectangle is shaded red?

2 Copy this rectangle and shade $\frac{1}{4}$ of it blue.

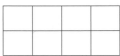

3 Which fraction is equivalent to $\frac{1}{2}$?

$\left(\frac{3}{8}\right)$ $\left(\frac{3}{4}\right)$ $\left(\frac{2}{8}\right)$

$\left(\frac{4}{4}\right)$ $\left(\frac{2}{4}\right)$

4 Write the next equivalent fraction.

$$\frac{1}{3} = \frac{2}{6} = \frac{3}{9} = \frac{\square}{\square}$$

5 What is $\frac{1}{4}$ of 20?

6 Copy and complete by writing < or > between these amounts.

$\frac{1}{10}$ of 20 $\square$ $\frac{1}{2}$ of 20

7 Write $\frac{3}{10}$ as a decimal fraction.

8 Complete the fraction addition.

$$\frac{3}{9} + \frac{2}{9} =$$

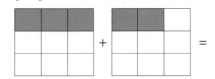 + =

9 Which fraction is equivalent to $\frac{1}{6}$?

$\left(\frac{6}{10}\right)$ $\left(\frac{2}{3}\right)$ $\left(\frac{2}{12}\right)$

10 Copy and shade $\frac{2}{5}$ of this rectangle.

11 Write the common fraction **and** decimal fraction for the missing number shown by the arrows.

0   1

12 Write these fractions in order, starting with the smallest.

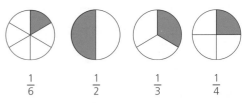

$\frac{1}{6}$ $\frac{1}{2}$ $\frac{1}{3}$ $\frac{1}{4}$

13 Complete the fraction addition. Use the image to help you.

$\frac{1}{5} + \frac{3}{5} =$

+ =

14 True or false? $\frac{1}{3} > \frac{1}{4} > \frac{1}{10}$

15 Copy and complete this equivalent fraction chain.

$$\frac{1}{5} = \frac{\square}{10} = \frac{3}{\square} = \frac{4}{20}$$

16 $\frac{1}{10}$ of 50 =

> **There are 36 balloons in a pack.**
> **Write the number of each type of**
> **balloon for questions 17–20.**

17 $\frac{1}{2}$ are red balloons   =

18 $\frac{1}{3}$ are green balloons =

19 $\frac{1}{6}$ are blue balloons   =

20 $\frac{1}{4}$ are large balloons =

42

Score ◯ **/ 20**

1 A glass holds 250 ml. How many glasses can be filled from 1 litre of milk?

2 A purse contains six 20p coins. How much money is in the purse altogether?

3 How many 500 ml jugs will fill a 3-litre bucket?

Look at the mug and spoon for questions 4–6.

70p   40p

4 How much does it cost to buy a mug and a spoon?

5 How much does it cost to buy five spoons?

6 How much change would you get from £3, if you bought three mugs?

7 What time does this clock show?

8 A cake costs 95p. Which four coins could be used to pay for it?

9 $1\frac{1}{2}$ kg = _____ g

10 Read and write the mass on each of these.

11 Three desks, each 150 cm in length, are put together to make one long table. What is the total length of this table?

12 Write <, > or = between the measurements for each of these.

2 cm ☐ 20 mm

50 ml ☐ 5 l

13 Which three coins make 25p?

14 Write the time shown on each clock.

15 4 m = _____ cm

16 How much money is this?

17 What is the total mass on this scale?

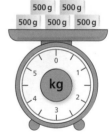

18 How many weeks is a 14-day holiday?

19 What is the time in half an hour?

half an hour later ⟶ ____

20 Which is longer, 18 cm or 81 mm?

Score ⬤ / 20

43

Published by Keen Kite Books
An imprint of HarperCollins*Publishers* Ltd
The News Building
1 London Bridge Street
London SE1 9GF

ISBN 9780008161224